the hauntRoad

KAREN GARTHE

spuyten duyvil
NEW YORK

©2018 Karen Garthe
ISBN 978-1-947980-37-2

Library of Congress Cataloging-in-Publication Data

Names:, Garthe, Karen, 1949- author.
Title: the hauntRoad / Karen Garthe.
Description: New York: Spuyten Duyvil, [2018]
Identifiers: LCCN 2018002270 | ISBN 9781947980372
Classification: LCC PS3607.A777 A6 2018 | DDC 811/.6—dc23
LC record available at https://lccn.loc.gov/2018002270

Designed by Ken Feisel. Cover image: detail from William Harvey's 1628
De Motu Cordis, courtesy Special Collections Archive, University of Liverpool

FOR CARLA

Meander if you want to get to town.
—Michael Ondaatje, *In The Skin of a Lion*

CONTENTS

...we should come back in the snow

- 17 *flag that saved a tribe*
- 18 **stringent**
- 19 scalloped
- 20 At the water
- 21 *middled in* THE SENDER
- 22 *Map...*
- 23 Limousined Boy
- 24 Red Rome
- 25 spent
- 26 Wild gray door
- 27 HORSESHOE

The mill snaps on its lights

- 30   Putnam Valley
- 32   Mill
- 3   Interstate
- 34   Trace Walk
- 35   yello brick
- 36   *at the bottom of the pines*
- 37   The Tar Porch
- 38   *Script of* a night's ocean
- 29   We run together
- 40   Striding the Depot
- 41   Comrade Train
- 42   Welsh Mine Sacred Heart
- 43   Golden Poverty
- 44   The Chandler
- 45   The Skipjack...
- 46   sharp Prow

Quest

50 *My Girl...*
51 Fool
52 Quest...
53 kiss whip
54 Her Terms
55 bolt empath
56 Sutra Heart
57 orthodox translucent
58 WILD WEST
59 Galaxy
60 **the shoulder of a darling...**
61 Presentation Bouquet
62 Aerialist
63 Minuet
64 *of all*
65 Coconut Coach
66 Elegy in "HR"
67 *I grip your hand so quickly,*
68 **striding The Henlopen**
70 Backbone Comet

Mercy build yer fires

- 74 *An off-the-shoulder* kind of Friday
- 75 Tristan Chord
- 76 **Denise's Party**
- 80 every embedded thing
- 81 *lollapalooza*
- 82 THE POUR
- 83 𝒵eitgeist, 𝓕ragrance
- 84 Compass
- 85 Tumult, Dear Tumult
- 86 Precision Bliss
- 88 the dream saw
- 89 the diamond is a square on point...
- 90 Landmark Weeping Beech
- 91 ON MY WAY TO YOU
- 92 *banners on high*
- 93 angel boots
- 94 door
- 95 THE **MEMORY** PALACE **OF** CHULA VISTA
- 99 Uphold. Protect.

- 101 Acknowledgments

...we should come back in the snow

*f*lag that saved a tribe

~
They were in Cairo like tiny cups of tea.　　He couldn't leave
　　　　　　　　　　　　　Her face　good bones he held
　　　　　　　　　　　　　　　　　　and kissed her eyelids,
the lightest part of cloud they were, such powers of everything

Still, they were rough and loaded.
The injured and fragile said *"back off."*

~
Red Rose, White Lily The Religious turn *while we tend their beasts*
　　　　　　　　　　　　　　　　　　　　different shapes usher,
　　　　　　　　　　　　　　shapes usher and circle
　　　Their wedding melts God

~
We demanded trick words STOP explaining ourselves STOP *I have taken my breasts and proffer them*. . .STOP laughing STOP
any annoying
　　　　Knowingness

~
The injured and fragile say *"back off."*

You have been treated gently, your own little diamond winking at your wrist
　　　　　　　　　　　　　　　　　　　　　　　keeps you
　　　　　　　　　　　　　　　　　　　　　fleet in air

17

stringent

    chrysanthemum   Tender
Cluster   *Blazed* composite thicket
Green hand terminus of the sound bell's
Gathering
    Mother Cone
    Blast
White
Peregrine   Doubt   Angel   curled   apostrophe
Pock
Wicker the
Thumb baskets of *most egregious throng*
Celebrity curmudgeon
Of undermining and
Grasping mistresses waving thru the rain quilt

Cymbal
Elegance of noblesse
Bushed sod bonnet   spidering oxeye globe
Mountain
Of cities on top of cities

scalloped

P oems hang in air boats and grammars of
   Mercy, it looks like
 she's in the night with stars, but
 she is in the sea with bright fishes she's in her Egypt bay

such shallow reasons   Why, some nights lay on the heart
                             like King David's musician
         harping,   scoring the ground   or he's home drunk
                  and super tired they lay   tensely mounding
   scalloped in the patter   of an uncertain horn

At the water

                p *l i s h* its small mirrors
                ethical color
                        R ose Red
          slim *fish*
        p *l i s h* : I want
          your ton of face
    age whitish around the eye
    net
    of fragile marine

Misunderstanding poetry, panicked and unconsoled
The persistent defeat you wear in the dream

                slim shelf poetic. . .gate that never was more still
                pale
                foot
                stake out
  the floor powders little crab-seared
                        meals & the procedural motions of tea
            e l a b o r a t e
            seconds
of everything richly prepared
&
the gate that never was more still

middled in THE SENDER

                                                        Started howling
                                                                LOVE,
                                                              By JOVE!
sweets the dry-down   spanse like NASA' trajectory hubbles stars
                         wisdoms
                of
                Elderly Animals BelloWLOVE
                the drunken daylights
                the smoothieVelvet. . .
                                  NOW:
Now. SUPPOSE. . .just SUPPOSE   *you   even   <u>Have</u>*   LOVE
                                      LOVE like blown showers
                                you have
the clever foxes' known many and you have the hedgehogs' known one
                pile empire   surely ripening grapes the wisdoms, those
                      Elderly
                            just start *howling*
                                  LOVE's *all serial and oatsie. . .*
                                harts in the fir needles
              running down the stores of snow
                                    LOVE Is
Married All His Life   & he Cant *wheedle free or even die*
        (for that matter
dark
        scare pods by the million's) by *JOVE*, LOVE gets
trap-sprung
        n'*all Dovey* of *sucre*-like-Pearl
puffs Cinnamon **& Eye** of Horn   **some times**
                thriving so capably
                          & LOVE's howling
                children do
drop off safe to sleep

                                                                                        NEWTOWN, 2012

Map
of the ocean floor

                                  the mid-Atlantic Ridge, the
sunk palace of Cleopatra in a shallow   Egypt Bay's
                                              reach the
                                Old Saws
                                         Rebekah at her well
misers'   dashing   star   orchestra   &   ladders
                                          like Jack's
                                        stalking
                                        Gold
Blistering   the ash floor's diabolical wetness
as having failed the threshold
as mauve exhale dinging the steps, the falling up and down
                        hydraulics
                                of neon-reamed bottles of wine

forgive the bravado they have they have *this Beauty Shade of blue*
                always somewhere   somewhere
                                on their person

Limousined Boy

a limousined boy and the *Kyrie* under everything dwells at the

waterline or puzzles

the limousined boy havened warm in the back seat, usher

his *Kyrie* Youth

purrs the boy's mobile restrained tint, placid as tabled water

as olives tasting the peaceful mouth

a wandering beam of boy his limousine housing safe progress

Red Rome

*Let's go in out of noon's cowlick,
out of long greens towing the plaid wake...*

Here's our lounging clemency
Trot luck in this wild life we'll keep to
                  our margin palazzo
    make friends with the cook's patient
reddening shards

  we walk on
  the edge of
The city   "between worlds without exchange or recognition...
                           so severe as to be vertiginous"

                      and console
              This
      glassine birdsong and Rodeo Red Rome
When the sun goes down and toys the top of fire

                    spent

              blue *cheques*
         the   piazza   air   pure baby of the blue
                            storied
                            Virgin

                              Alouette
          crossing   the Wake in bobbed piazza air...

  we should come back in the snow
                         ease her down in the crook of your arm
                                              the promenade stripes
                              the Crane Stairs
                              whisk

     (Ahhh...*You'll never best the Italian with his half and half nobility*
       all   the suppurations of his beads'
                        la forza

      we should
       come back
      in the snow
  ease her down in that mob that drowns the world

Wild gray door

    BY Thee

        pulling curtains back to the blowing grasses

                I'd not repair the peeling
        paint or augment
        the sloping
          tilt
          broke cups
newspapers at night for blankets for warm
              daisies outside this wild gray door

HORSESHOE

        ringing warehouse
           keeps its prime panels and vault   *the revoked*
loft mound of luminous hash savings
                I find her gentle. . . pushing ominous clouds away
                    cross-legged, folding interiors

    the last time you stayed awake watching parking sparkle in trees
  a private serenade dissolved I can sleep here, *I can fall dead to the public*
     and ask the carpet of half stones and
           shells   wigwam sapling bum wanderers

        thunder
   a horseshoe covered with anything
unbeknownst in some old fort tandem ordinary and push along the peace,
  a kind of
horseshoe coddling bait orchard
   with peaches in soldier half light and a pure dark unknown

The mill snaps on its lights

Putnam Valley

                          Hi Sleigh dome
                            the buff valley's
                                   blindLake
                          shivers the
     ScaleTwerp of persons rake undercloud   *Cry Cry* planet chords

     barreling holiday grog
                     plunge
          the frack
     grade buff   water table   c r e ek as the devil is fallow
                                                              we're joyful
                     coronet and engine whip the road
     Glacier
     rock part
            sorties of natural iteration
     that the stock well sheep   the family

                                                twigs   all   night
                           the hauntRoad

                 choosing its future girl   cracked *substrate*
                                                        loll forest
                            loll Her   peanut beige   Her
                                      true exploration
                 tongue
                 the precipice every crest has

                          fanfare traffic   We Carts Pin Dolls
                             lamp flags
                             the   LateShift
                                        Digs
          hot   medals   team accomplish takes

    the bridles of lead   *ponies*
                               shifting,

          hoove

                    the forest

            floor
                    n' go
            *D*eeper than these But These
*A*re some of the hues that swing the dark

Mill

        this canopy of sycamore splays a feel bond   *The End*
                                                      Of SummerinTheEye
                     the breezed *final*
                               governor
                                                  flourish

                                    rapt
      lyric gasping
              Perfume.
              Costume.
              Promise.
A very very *high shade*
of birds but not the birds themselves. . .

              a breeze blows the water wheel so   now THE MILL
SNAPS ON ITS LIGHTS

lovely pear blossoms aisle & the fanged bark soothes to a ribbon
                                                soothes "to a man"

but the shaft of birds drives back in the tight airless part of wounds they lock

                    they   tuck   in
  the breast
    of an old personal street

Interstate

                                          When was the last
                syncopated zigzag down
                    the The Cherrystone Casino's
          beggarly pinnacle
                              TIGHT ROPE   *forestly dark*
   inside travel pouring
                    summer corn
                    kitchen kiss
         the luggage of lonesome's
I Don't Carewreck   that Christ-raised talk liveries High
                              Flowerfull Air
garlands bronco brokenness   the rag plastic angel waving high up in the tree

Trace Walk

      moving South, mounding the interstate minor scale
                                                swamp bowl
                                                    rowing
              smoking ashes b*lowback*
         mesa
                Indian   Ground   TraceWalk *Listening to the dark all*
      your robbers are
  listening too

creatures chitter   the Pale *In-BetweenSpirits* harrowing inches above ground
stepping their Halo walk   moving
                          South, how honey hardship seals
                                     immersed   en trapped

    Trace without electrics to squelch and exceed the stars
all prey all preying
raw throats pitch *no being goes into nothingness*

yello brick

bread smells sweet
its tender lasts *a wink*   *I'll take in hand*
this whole yello brick
sustained the dirt poor
Southern

Marmoreal of my death walk's matchless
isolation zeal
froze pain
I'll read   the German Family
once again   crammed with voices
annoyance   love
the material
faith
fright
     Cozy This
yello brick bread I bake lights
my death walk lifts *fragrance*
   of mignonettes lining
   the beds
   ebbed
and flowed on the breeze

at the bottom of the pines

        the gleam of the copse hammock
        shaft shower dive
        upturned faces cruise
        the mercy taps all day *Savoy*
        ocean
        kudzu tightropes drip
        I'll never do it again swags
   or compact like hens on squares
she looks like a little Shepherd but who knows what she is
        through the gold lock of trees
        she's forestall aftermath
        grudged through the drawer for a smoke
        at the bottom of the pines
        children blind the still's iron
        legs *orange-ing* the grass
        gale
        kindling
        at the bottom of the pines

The Tar Porch

              W*ine to the lips*   scandal forming
    little pools in the sides of a mouth's
                         Oyster-soft sympathy

to night's get – up – cold – bath stars   *glisten the tar porch*
the dark split poems reel

Script of a night's ocean

                       Comfort of pepper dogs   joy in the woods
   and a moonshine sip handing back the lost understanding of I*mposter*
                                            on the rim of the flavor deal's
                                            shakedown

                     performance of experts'
  *fleece*Soft   remoteSlaughter
                  The Peace Fountain's
             metal   L*ot*
                 R*ubble* Tots sift
hard futurestones

   alms bucket foundlings of the kind soldiers swing
   black money
   breeding
something you feel walking around ((like spirits in the rich artist's loft, whose little gods trip. . .

                                      I Dream ofYOU,
                             your each note lifts
                the albatross asleep on grains of night
    flocking like swifts *re f*orm the airscape
        keenly sift
        unison detail

      clinking
Our tumblers in the woods downwind of the smokehouse
purring words blocky and knocking and sitting on Paradise Hill

We run together

                We never
        left
           our *life on the spear end*
glinting its point
a scar   pressuring
thru the sieve we leave our jackals

                          Behind the veil
                     you   *are*
          pure *love* ringing
my hands a font
        for
the thirsty losing angel whose wing caught
shouting down the door
totalizing silence

we run together

Striding the Depot

                        Cassandra's pronouncing now,
                skating 'round her Vision Room
Vulcan's tortured plasma steals
            ripe redness, every bit of *louche*
in a World Choral *Photographie*
                  Axe Tongue
                  Mash
                  Soliloquy
                            One table that holds enough
            is what you have   sugar, tea, an egg
            a football loaf tucked underarm
striding the depot, the brow of professional everything
but
ONE table holding enough is what *you have, you have that crust*
of football tucking the Homecoming
                          meat pie rheumatism
                      tongs to the fire
everything awaits
            Cassandra's scintillate
            Scout Honor
the sequined terminus of fame's just-birthed-bird havoc
and way out on a limb
the echo wood's protective
            gears and cogs   Echo
                    little dovetailed snakes   the
                          Mustang Extinction
                          Address

and Art *Talk* in The Business Model Cassandra moves into
the Aquadome
seeding clouds

Comrade Train

Velocity couplet, trine harpoon of *those who feel each other*
                                                     ellipsis
                                              and   so   on
                    and so on   the down low
Easy arm insouciance that butters the device now swarms the bench
                                        in digit trim

                                Calls

                                        The children

                                        Safe Home
The fume-end of heirloom occlusion quivering
                                        the lips
                                of the Comrade
                        Train's
        toggle mouth and face   **electric**
                                untouchable
                                sizzling
        moonlight trinkets
        light the eyes

Welsh Mine Sacred Heart

      Taped-up faking
     love joyed-over-the-grave underfoot
  slips
clenching love
   joyed all over so far up over the normal range there's **fatigued**
  Love, Joy Blood sugars So Low that NOW MEAN LOVE
gets right up close
      (&
     the black-faced miners sing out of the mines they sing the
     whites of their eyes black dust befallen they sing for their wives
     and children they sing for themselves in the Old Welsh-mastered
     tones)
screeching **Gull Gurls'** play dead murder sound
winding sheets right at you
the fibrous wind coaxing
the surnamed tendrils
         strung out in your damp cave suffering
           preside
         Children,
Children,
sing for yourselves in the Old Welsh-mastered tones!

Golden Poverty

but a home that warm brick-brown-cells the Oak the Brass **the *fluid* oak**

hide of the public house   oh clay silt venting   a Private Fold **silken means**
Means Victory legions cede
                              ***h*eritage** legs Fall Down Ghost Purchase

the ghosts talk how good they are   they can marigold warm lamps icy silver and
enable such **Golden Poverty**   they *sink*
                              pink cradles down the blast **and scald**
sea birth: *Here Whites The Afterlife*
all done

at ecstasy *d*one
at misery in the cowshed misery on the beach The Body of Love *all done*

quarantine Lip of a shelf of *lazareti*   at the water's edge **Quarantine**
       Close
       Body quiver   love light **anneal and quarantine** the little hope bells
       voweling red inside the breast
fluid

oak and brass predator panic all the panic run prey

The Chandler

                        pins back a diving foil *thinning beautifully*

Whistling Chandler whose fire tongs go *donning, tempting*
                                                        vamping
                                     the Symbol of a Symbol
                   (if you want to Go Beautifully, **Go.**
              Wine Torn Bath
                 kit n'caboodle of True

Recluse   *imagine you know this ghost witherships bring to bear*
boxed white suns bring to bear   the ground and all the Air Families cohere
                              dark tenants
                         dank ropes of hair memorial-cut like Caesar
The adventures of the townhouse
decline
       of Whores and Rough Riders who *flee reck*oning

            (each of two text messages
               upsets a different way   the pirouette wobbling
                   affect
boring
deep kissing the body and the ground

          The Skipjack
              . . . this fluffy pond of head in hand

                The Skipjack's low freeboard
         guzzling
   vistas Setter Sail   moon ropes the bottom
                                        cavalcade

Trench goblet of a particular *flavor* song lapsed in the cold asthma air

Holds
all present & absent turns   thrown
under the bus

          Then
grabbing backward, selecting final clothes
                                 to thread your wandering
                Skipjack & navigate
its rollshape baskets creaking
     GroundWater in cold asthma air
  I   lay down on
      The   Skipjack's low Freeboard Keep

sHarp Prow

Fan
satin lips of water drape   a   long   veil
                   b r e a s t i n g the   LONE
boat   in   the   darkNight Beam
gray-faced   gray *swindling*
                wisps off the water strokes
                           rowing
                              lone
                                figural
mound mount and spear rim   coasts to the edge of the world
                        swoon oars *stirring*
                          delicate night
                       delicate peace
What we'd do with such a starred   *clear chance*. . .
               a satin crossing
               a long kiss
                   of darkness
        shrouding   enemies
        shrouding bedlam day

Quest

     My Girl
       leading
      Eurydice

        her forearm crooning
        these many
        Caves/Shelters
        brighten straight to
     My Girl wings
    an empty bowl

    when baptism comes down she
  closes her eyes
      in her own counsel
     her own town of sextant knives and cigar beard suppers

in and out Caves/Shelters these many
Stir

             Eurydice

Fool

I repair fast, but spheres
                    of countless shame bells

    stride limitless beheading

ACORN AT DAWN, the Pink/Gold rule of pinch hours

               Fool Blue Air *O Beautiful Path!!!*

Indecent orbits of Cruel Streaks run their powers

    The glittering pipe snakes of Masters

                              & the miserable
                    flute
    girls of gender corn whose babes gurgle sleep

Quest

(if the mints are poison

Little Sinecure governess come face to face with her master, two trumpets
Greet the dawn of
His little lambs)

Unenchant me off the pony charm, gait   Unenchant me from the veils
poles
your charges' iron field-thru scatter
unenchant   but please do not dissolve me
          Leave something

     of me
       . . .something left

          I have covered and misled, I have
stated your formula and your long practice   Please Unenchant Quest

rising and neighing
impatient for its ride to redress

       my robe's
          Broider
             I am Ancient
                 leave something of me, little
         sinecure
         elegant spore of profession

kiss whip

pillowed *Inward*

Now a brick in the bride of itself
 tight ropes, teeth nets

sodasteps fizz
 night bundling tigers purr
 their exotic and their restraint
 "She's a feast," they say

and then they say *"but he's the solarium incubates*

our gold"

Her Terms

of a
brush with the deeper tendons

    taut
       silence

((((Cream fluff of affection my feeling is sweet and lumbered and drowsy In Cave
in *cave, cave, cave* BEWARE Her

                          artifacts *turn over the earth*
                                       Her Terms
          of
      Beauty *cut   down   the   whole   forest   of   my   people*

cabling shrouds
    graft Their Creature

their stark tear sheath

bolt empath

                              the ground shifts
                         his gift
        skipping over mines by instinct
                                    discretely
                     aerates and *communes*
        trolls his own violence
        tickles his own geography
                he'll bolt
        like the phantom *he* is
                          He Is
                    t**h**e **f**ather *handsome rogue*
leaving everyone   straining for presence

Sutra Heart

Now that the old brides are in hospice under quilt drip speech...

                                           *P*arsifal ------cosseted *B*lunderer.

Thirster.
      The canary in the mine is crying a common cinema of the image

How much like the Symposium is Genji's tale?   The polis sits around talking:

               you have changed your body inside and out

        My friend   old brides quilt drip
    Speak the reverie aisles they came down

veils, cusps
Parsifal ------cosseted Blunderer.

     Sew up the flap-jack valves

astonish grooms

fine love hands

             orthodox translucent

                    sock polishing the old beige suspension
              corridor
of elite   blooms   this Hospital of Aria and Vermeer
rainbow
carrot
whole body health
          . . .a very great old age of orthodox translucence
                                        is willow-bent in bed
                                     his son's helping him
                                  pale eth*er* wh*ite* ste*ams*
                    their black dot caps, they are their own oak
but "mine is the cocoon of the crone" feather suspension, her
tall bed
boat alone
          somersault in the lungs and grip of The
          Warlock of infamous   unknown   vintage
          floods
                sherries   of relief
finishing   in the arms of strangers

WILD WEST

                              to the river sunset blinds
               the *beveling water*
                              right there You are
a soft grotto curved at the top of Old Glory painted on the floor
                                    my Futureworld
                                             of
                                        Man Down

              Dream Girl who cares when you die   *arching Old Glory*
                           your jailBlack Cross *hacking*
                                         l *urching*
                 drunken blood orange   whips   and ruin

                                              Finally
                    the last lodge, great snow   Mountain
      V*iew sledged in the arms of the good long wife*
                            the kind drug waltz
                     and the tv's blooming scarf of pale
                                                  country music

Galaxy

                    Squeezing, tightening the juice out
         forgiving nothing, not mother with her dying totals,

    or the working papers sag in humidity

            The door seeping
THIS IS THE COLOR OF MINE EYE, HALO ITS GALAXY   OF ROBBED DESCENT

    night air moistens   . . .Sumptuous   . . .Decay

    my hair and clothes are soaked & tangle
                           I was here
                                padding down the hall, clocking the doors
                 I was
fondling small change, heating up the dimes

reach in the world from the bed's dying totals

the shoulder of a darling
SUN HERALD

                      Unaccustomed nomad
      sun struck in space without skin
                            (or skin's gone, and liquidity asks

   to settle the self on a residence dune, the shoulder of a darling

architecture of feeling pendulums,   cool neutralities
     Bless   *Repeat Bless*   OTHERWISE, *to such a tremendous*
                                Unluck
                                Angel
DO NOT say things lightly, otherwise he'll lob
                          Atmosphere, mug a Twister
                      portray the outcome waves

At the shoulder of a darling   *the cool neutrality of repeating*

dunes
mansion-talk, gallery-speak set the social porch   jewelling
                                          under the belfry
                                        fan
palliative   as able tiny
         sea lovely basket stars   (but I don't wish them to be
                                        so salty. . . so cold
                        this milky way
       hallucination brings *more odes to the Ears of Luck*
                more wreck flowers
              ultra-violet
                a barbarous mattress
                    set out to dry

Presentation Bouquet

Mt. Wilson's great lens is hatching   *the tempest of a star's departure*

another's *sizzling* **phenomena**   then, *a new star's raw natal ascent*

                      The Envies sit around and slap

                      hot dust, cosmic eiderdown hovering
       this Eye of darkness...

             WAIT...just N *ow the coast's* clear...

the avenue swings a breathy pendulum

nighttime castles of the homeless hunker and pull in merciful air

the great lens is hatching celestial, heavenly presentation bouquets

                      mighty rods, tulip chalice

End Time Bundling   our animals, our T*rophy* Eternal*fang*Horn
                         skinfused industrial   ...*God bless us*
                         senseless
pig cow ashes mix with mine, the science aria
                         rings

                         conviction from the helicopter
rotary thrown rain

Aerialist

not everybody gets to break in a virgin ceiling on a tensile swath
bundling and unbundling
yearning

pastie rounds, eye patch dousing
shocks of silk
the knees gulf

not everybody gets to ramp up the mulberry gear and wink
the great divide
cocooned in the iceberg calving

Minuet

*f*alling upward cinched at the waist a little tornado

     Vortex of VisibleWind

  or
 dawn only
First Light *only* minced artifice as upward fell
       the heavy cowards vigor dolls
  jolly Mariah all of the dainty
escaped

from stone
ringlets
lace pleas'
     toile of falling upward
      to the boil core of dance dream
     flakes
   and powdered peace

of all

                  graciously entubed private mists
bowers of category arch the flora
of my congested arms
      & *slide*
the hip of my animal fuselage
rests in lathers chemically

loading and unloading

manufacture's starvation equalities

Coconut Coach
(at the plural of midnight

H*OtBat* Kill   gluey swelter so
Dress White... think
of the forest in loose green shadow,
think **Ban Fire**, ban
the hammer heat coal's shrie k dar k

THINK just think of forest*L*oosegreen
the grateful soldier you gave your pantry humility,
you gave
all Your
Thanks...

P*lum White GrapeWhite*
Coconut Coach Prince Mohammed sidles up to me at the plural of midnight

dedicated safe
Dress White
tempo of house music's monotonous chambers
a grace climate
f alling
q uenching
b anning fire *We* P*rocess*
plural midnight
glide the pulse of surcease

Elegy in "HR"

        with the soft sag skin, sallow
demure with her cane prissed between her knees
and knocking on a glass bowl with a spoon
one spoon of whole millet at a time
                        we have a little almost peace now, we have
           the loving smell of boxwood green

We Have the distance between complaint and whining noticing and unnoticing
taking up and putting down to take up and gain again
another abundance
           of side-by-side equivalencies

        DEAR PEEVISH MYSTIC, *Let us review*
           how light we might make them seem
this litter of satellites, pseudo stars **black sails requiem**
priss between knock knees
the glass bowl sails for help and other gusts of mercy

I grip your hand so quickly,

                    in the deeps of the train dead heat cooks
             some Poor Dear's penned-in enterprise
                                     GUITAR clopping
                             dusty Western
                           fistful under Citicorp
       ....*Look! There's merry*
There's merry-eyed as tonic Muddy Water's
                          man like sugars must be
                    Excellences. . .
                     &
               Healings
               *R*efunds
in loneliness the tunnel rings, I grip your hand quickly
                        "I want you to be everything
              & eternally
cheat sheet the devils of our face
train clangs and custody
become
a queen of dream

striding The Henlopen

                                          The Striptease of poverty sly peels
      her
          jacket   a side to show   HER GUN WINs
                                          sashays   all the choke
                                                          debt
                                                      sprinkling
                               grease fat flags
   cars parts
     all over   the nothing-to-do-sky
                                                    At this moment
                  a small gold
drops inheritance
                  & a hotel's loose-off-white
                                                watered aqua
               slides over
the Sand   Wreath
     Peninsula   sun's all prosper & lifting   across
                                                               the
                                                                Hotel
                                                                   tile,

                                                                                   trousers

                                                                           glide

                      slow f a n s **scent**   **a pardon**

(**whispers the ocean**

               sluice   this   moment's peak   stucco *and salt*
                                     krystals The Old Crest delicately

            The Intaglio Embleming

                                           Ttremors

&Y*elps* Right **here** beauty's   loved   again

Backbone Comet

          Brakeless
      taper to the boulevard
         fling open
              *j***OY** she said
  arrow this
waterhorse
backbone comet   *Why, you are just*
  the rolling export of The Joy mate,
     Boom Ahoy! Swim
        right over
           the math
             skill
        barter no measure
   just bend
round
clamor
              Come along,
   now swallowing chevron dynamo
         blades glinting blades
     tight
      squeeze by near miss service roads
   width
uncivil jungles
Blow This
    hydrate the wrinkle
   song
  hang in
smog's lung awfuled shape
             F l i n g (damn!)
          Open **J**oy
   brakeless taper she said
  B<small>LO</small>W <small>TH</small>IS
    quarreling hive

Mercy build yer fires

An off-the-shoulder kind of Friday

Take her *start diva* glittering
                    arrow pearl smoke
        chats up channels *sorrow, sorrow, sorrow*
        for these
        the Lord of Compassion keeps

                              his crown
                            flaming

        his serene triangle prayer

    Is he lonely?   Yes.   Have all the
days of timeless

    wear rattled initiatives
   fathomed Great
Works
Fandangos' entire
   fluid swish?

                The Lord of Compassion….is he
                lonely?

                        Yes.
                    SWish.

every topcoat brakes the sidewalk
    under violent lights
We're all awake
We're having a party that will not end in years

Tristan Chord

        we *were* a soulful bunch   needed *Everything*
              ((though we *needed* NOT speed,
                      . . .*needed* NOT money

        we had
        Tristan's chord *B*elting
    T̲h̲en
  E̲arth S̲tood
no futurethought more than ourselves, our diamond
splintered all over the nighttime floor
                            we   shed   honey   tears
                                  & we shunned the morning light, hey
we clocked in at midnight and laughed ourselves alive

we were just bouquets of wanting each other in the smoke blue strata
                                                hovering
                                           hovering
        the roiling tint of Tristan's chord **we needed**
no resolution more than ourselves

Denise's Party

                                                                                     New ice

                                                                     another
                                                                     verse
in its special envelope *wafting thru the Day Laws,*
                                       or,
                                                     as Japanese things are
such *Thick Obedience of the all figured out*
Or: it's just your average pain rocking back and forth on her heels

                Whereupon beads of anguish take her
                        start up the bunny hill
                        cross country

                        (we are the finest skaters
                                  of
                           New Ice
                         We ARE the very Least Friction

core and sample baseline *she doesn't want to lose her husband*
                                but we're so far into Jersey
                            now. . . your Perfect Navy
                            knits
                                    a   bridge,

    Twill Girl with a big fat book got wet
ripples pages got the covers tear Oh, let it be
cloves rapture indestructibly or let it be Leakey-like
stages of human summary rake over the edge
evolution girl
crossing aisles
with a fine diagonal drinkThen a third
snuggling her coat she
sits right down before me Two
of the three wear pearls culture they are
So good at
just like the steam is
gorgeous and   Bellows in freeze   cold   air,

slurp

Nothing's yours...not the dog   the baby   or the walls of man

  not the names of ownership wield

     the lengthy soprano   warring   sure sure sure sure right right
                right yeah yeah yeah right yes yes absolutely
         anything less doesn't make sense
         for my money or my time

       It was righteous, then it was conflict...then it was mourning
      It was personal
     Sorrow
    Still

True! True!
nubby glasses wear their shoes out on the lip
& orange/Irish whip up
stirs
& hobnobs that picture of weary suffrage
              my good farm girl
                  my wifey to the wick
      grizzle drunk
          in
        clink ice
         if I even bother with   *ice...*
the amber Fury Slurp
the keys fumble
  hall,

<pre>
                         The *Jazz M*essenger

                              He said *I don't like Tchaikovsky*
                           valve trumpets runnel
*V*elvet chairs dying heart scrapes he said I'm hungry he said I can't
                  make this trip without food
I shall enjoy every minute of your departure
                      *b*eginning the End ratting its dry can, then
                                       soaked
                                       withall
swell erotic tuck-ins
      For *this is the Jazz Messenger*   who happens only at night
horning his can unto brass

      NOW,   **is not S***lver* **The Lace Sound poets** take over the water
under the sharp mural stars, Desert Father agoras and buccaneer brite lite
                                      ?
                                (indeed. . .*IT IS*
                                   but
it is also. . . beginning the End) **That Linden Spangling**
her Giantess at the
          window
                  &
                               The Jazz Messenger's cooling trailing
      lullaby *J*oy the Earthworks   *J*oy the potato fields

           King balloon
                      of the triangle
                      Christmas I lost you
                      Kansas, Kansas backs
                   ONE FARMHOUSE LOFT ONE
      Girl*M*om with her bottle
      window perched Lookout
      on the river the Fishers dip
      King balloons
         raise-up
            the loft flags
               tenderness
</pre>

                every embedded thing

            mossfurred gully to the back door, Charm House
            vining the alley's sweet nature**r**ot**M**oist
                            Night decay
                       The *rougeNOir* way IN
    the florid lay-about firebrand's pleasure breath   tho
                       NO MORE FAME, NO GALVANIZING MYTHS anymore
                                            than an embroidering Ukraine
                firebrands TO**r**ch   the songs the singer presses
    her *gimlet kiss, her samba on horseback's* Full Set of Standards hold
    every embedded thing

lollapalooza

     Ceramic made to hold in Formal Loss
bone on the dollar wind   wind on
the browbank   a kitten *seeking its own* mewling
in the see-thru   shafts   driven Mesmer
    driven
    stride
my train of shabby gown

my SugarPelt dragging a mash aisle
    dragging Her

   small gal skeleton thru *don't think I didn't*
notice **The Lollapalooza's** caly*pso* red *edge*
       its Joy-ruffed sleeve
                jostling the backroom assassins

THE POUR

                                        of see-thru
                                    the stash of composure
                    a piece of coughing
            crumbled
    down the tin bar
twinkling pastels, brown bourbon tricks
fix the hands
reach nouns, touch verbs throwing sparks   *setting*
                              all the doll varnish aflame
rocking, davening in front of the mirror
                              words gold fish
                pretty rhetorical cause, great meaning
              lying-in-state
          on shallow cushions
joy
and bliss not a moment too soon

Zeitgeist, Fragrance

A Great Actor plays
himself *Crushed in God*
under the eyeArch inside-out Man in Man Asylum wick
fire straw
heaps the zeitgeist of this fragrance wheezing reeds
whistling temple sweat
nosegays of precipice in silky tumbler's
        rue
his bride
loves
unconditionally
melts the Hollywood glade
        the driveway-wide
thunder door and lemon wax
linoleum with its poignant mound of kids

Compass

Someone ferries back,   ruches the slip
piles hang together & mound all the
               DiscoDead
          ecstatic night's
       crazed socket dock

            my caveat rerun BROKE: *Emph*atically BROKE

the lines got cut, knots sloop and creep (*Oh, Mercy build yer fires*
the clang posts, the piers. . .
every which way you go a jury strafes the bones

Tumult, Dear Tumult

                                        East to West the sky was shuddering
              old-fashioned dying *30 Nembutals and a plastic bag*
                                              but Tumult,
                                              Dear Tumult,
                                              I was serene
                    hear Ye see Ye
                               Next anybody thumping so
                                    and properly soft
                                                          mannered
                                              I tranquil*ed*

                                     DOVE   HIGH OVER

                                        THE SPAN
                                              East to West
the sky shuddering if we're not alone or if we are   vaults *If you disappear*   *If*
              you vanish. . .
I felt for the bridge of the underbelly, Tumult
                                    Firm
                                    *M*aterial beside you

              the brass kiss glistens
              habit flecks deliquesce   and whisk by
              they beat everyone hard now

       hear Ye drum
   rain sounds so. . .
   Ye throw down trees

Precision Bliss
to WLO

He Did All
the reaching in assemblies
strangling
*f*undamentalism
He tossed
the cherry stones...... crushed cans in the ice plot of his own
inconceivable child
stumbling   waving He did
all the cooking   lurching
casting
plates to that small pine square
that chip on his shoulder   Long John's parrot barbarian of inner combat
a   thousand   mile   stare
of precision bliss   the whitest sky
in a fulsome rotting cream r
Painte*P*ainting
the cold glare behind the cross
finished in gilt
at the foot of the bed

He Was blue-veined as a stevedore,
John Henry driving
hammering
for
artist
gazillionaires
was
so very taken   by that little   Paris   *Lace*   *Marm*   Koronet &
raptor to her toes
commanding   **Buff The Bar**   **Burnish the spindles**......*Darling*

Nighttime's epicures likkered & saddled-up Grandly
Soho   *sans memory or scale*
the bar was
their horizon,

      THE NEW YEAR   *f*ickled rain
                           the Holland
                            Tunnel sagged
                      in
the highway running   its sneak of cars

                                the dream saw

                                                      1) Ships. *Overnight*.

                            I can see the Little Tawdry
                    awning Her Spiritual
             daze concrete

              who drank every struggle is different from the one who didn't. . .skin
        shifts   girt
                sit with me in the shadows

for a minute, topple the nonsense, *pick up*   *between the littleawning scrapes*
for so long at windowless interiors your eyes are attempting headlights
the thousand mile stare

banging into the shelves and inscrutably flinching screens
you just don't
know
until it happens

to   you

He Advances The Dream Saw   only Irish
                            encrypts
                                        the
                                    bones
tangled in **the fly rod briskly Protestant**   little red awning Her Chaos
is tongue stiff
blood in the breeze Ships.   *Overnight*.   Skybox the game.

the diamond is a square on point,

        Gardenia

        let the dog in
he's cold & use the apple
Any
Way
weather no method, Gardenia. . .*he's cold*

      so   *serious boats can be made*
palms plank together
little fingers pull steam & breathe
the wayward round, round
        let the dog in, Gardenia
& set out a bird tongue about the Holly Fool

Landmark Weeping Beech

                      hobs Easter   balloon stakes the flat
             scholastic of Natives here...
            then wealth here...then, the fervor
       gripping   nuns   now buried   Sisters' whole corps
at the feet of a rough *Pietà*   maids under stone *long live Resurrection*
                           Hearts
                    carved *in tree*
          and birds light *the crown of this*
hobbed one   weeping the sward Now   a lot of cars and deliveries here
                                at the edge of *TheAfterlife* crest's
                                            cascading apron
                      a great domed curtain *gownstreaming*
              throbbing   upside-down trumpet of deeper story
     flying about the trunk and the crown
   darts birds
febrile stripe and row these   cars   and deliveries
                   Sun Wealth chirps
                     the weeping
                        beech

ON MY WAY TO YOU

       When in the grainiest black and white I remember
the white lace shawl of the villain beauty is
mineral ground metal dirt
crops of the bulls of the earth

       Out in mid-Ocean now *for* the party prospectus
Dutch settled and broke up the rocks
wagons fired the sky
naturally portraiture there Miss Winter fattens-up

       & I *glissade* the restaurants hapless heads down
dining Ministries of Chefs Royale *glissade*
cheap clothes blocks clothes block after cheap blocks on my way
to you straps of orchids stroke rams heads and pills of anxious decline

       Solder each link each hair-brain-helmet schemes
what Blue for my enclosure that very first mid-ocean I held
the rock all night it was still tight in my hand in the morning sparkle
on my way to you

banners on high

hand held out in the jade   fog of thick collapsing Felt Belief in light
not warmth   lightening stoked the jade fog You could see
dragons balloon up gullies in the rain   you could see   to sanction
you could get to the House in the Glass   towers and air booms
panorama
run free in the sky house You could   Be alone with air
ice tables and chairs that dis-invite as welcome
Great   banners on high
and talons of wind

angel boots

the lilies stand their dream open
white castanets of green possession
a lap Jesus and a leopard to stalk
the bright
end of the cave
murder shouts to the ferryman stirring his soup
and the cave withal dry scrabbling is
a shell to the ear
zillions sound

the wren causes the avalanche
the pinprick to fall off spinning
at the point of the sacrum
tears start
but the spine has angel boots
calcium nests and wing parts
mist *it must take years to return*
the integers and unknown sums
      to reckon
      gist
at night the angel boots sound down corridors
marble harangue

door

~~
The door in the love in the dark where nothing's separate
                                       is hinged and weighs
                     swording, draping
                 the door in the love *rosettes*,
   furls,   and under each furl is a shining middle sleep

~~
Think of   spooling
     lips to the brim in the mission part of brain
                     Bleeding
the reddest
    throat Pulse
       of V's Ventricle Hammock Love luxes   past
                                         the mouth
                                     the wall
                           of cordials sparkling
                           mirror backs

~~
Bounty the world.   I think I could fall in the pool where magnificence
                                                                             dips its talons
   but wander the margins dayHounds fetch to moon whinny
     the door in the love

THE MEMORY PALACE OF CHULA VISTA

                                                             Live Standup
Mannequin with painted hair   your face knotted in her apron sash
                 the tide laps up over
                            the track for the sliding doors
                                        (p.s. *the very best*
                                        Maryiinsky students
                               always got to water the floor)
             it pushes up the
             Parquet   a few songs *wobble*
                the death of news high in a silo in a distance
                                      to get to
but right here at sea level   I cover your face with kisses on the sleep porch   pilings creak
  like somebody singing All Beautiful Time
       morning drops on the bay
                so any dry leaf can take   Her on
                                                       our boats are hard
                                                        Fixed

A Purple Heart wants nothing to do with our starburst walk-on
                                  fountain-mouth of greatness,

                                                            mouth of our beginning
                                                        City beginning
                                                            the garbage is damp and cool
                                                            in its slum of female chords
            and lurid in the bookcase boys downy
                                                    sling   slap   tide
                        in the kitchen drawer   C-clamps, toothpicks
    Trojans left over from when we were kings

before we started living mother's death at table, hands folding nicely   on gray &   Yello
                                                Vinyl
        the buffet with cat statues on each side
                            &
        Enough Whiskey for everybody

    (a few little crabs dangle poolside)
                            Old Portuguese disaster boats weave
                                                                ship biscuit
The flint Sky Beggarland   of lava foremost
                                    rolls
Timbers swell
    The ballerina flogs her *pointes* on the master bath floor
                                                        Slamming Pure Form
                                softening   opening plush multiples
            of landowners in the guest bath

            of a luxuriant bedside fascination with miniatures   (*f* he really knows

                        anything like he says he does   or *f* he's just one more
            grinder under   the soundproof tile
                              quashing
                memory in the sash
of a woody plastic homemaker by the sea

My archers   my bear and my little cat roam free but Keep me in Sight *furled*
                in the curtains
                     on each side of glass doors sliding   To   Fro
                                                                        Islet
                                        Buried in the spellbound fog
                              in the Privilege of Silence
                              the Palace Swells

                    the sunshine horns of daylight
                  (all predatory males in plain sight)
    and Sleek By Water skiff jabbers   What*ever*
                                        We wish to ferry away
             (at a star's request)   When you set places at the table for your
                                            angels
                              don't forget to   Set a place for me

And keep thy heart light lest it make thee sink.
—Percy Bysshe Shelley, *Adonaïs*

                Uphold. Protect.

        Wade out&fetch the body, hon, Uphold.
                            Protect.

This could be our *Evermore*
        *Pa*stures of drugged towns, mountain   topped
                                     modal
Cuckoo sunset   vine-meld-trees and fossil spindled

                         porch tossed clods of boredom
                         the sun duets
           One in the Formality of The Other
(So, why, then, is the light at the **End** of the tunnel
Why not brightness
sitting here with us on top of the d*uet of One*
in the formalityof
The Other?
fabled in the satchel of trees
               so I say   *ahhhh, isn't that you, hon*
       I hear

           Uphold. . .

        wade out
    n' fetch the body

ACKNOWLEDGMENTS

With grateful thanks to the editors of the following publications in which these poems (or versions) first appeared:

AMP online: scalloped, Striding the Henlopen, Angel Boots, Precision Bliss

Aufgabe: Flag that saved a tribe; My Girl, leading Eurydice

Caliban online: The Skipjack…*this fluffy pond of head in hand*; Denise's Party; ON MY WAY TO YOU; orthodox translucent; Banners on high; TraceWalk; Presentation Bouquet, Mt. Wilson; Script of a night's ocean; Mill, Wild West (kind drug Waltz); We run together

Colorado Review: Limousined Boy

Court Green: Aerialist

Denver Quarterly: an off-the-shoulder kind of Friday; Landmark Weeping Beech; The Pour, Minuet

Flag and Void (online): THE MEMORY PALACE OF CHULA VISTA

FENCE: Welsh Mine; The Shoulder of a darling, SUN HERALD

Lana Turner, A Journal of Poetry and Opinion: Quest; Fool, Tumult, Dear Tumult; middled in THE SENDER; At the water; Elegy in HR; *I grip your hand so quickly*; Red Rome

New American Writing: Sutra Heart; HORSESHOE; Comrade Train; every embedded thing

Café between wars, chapbook (Red Glass Books, 2014): Fancy; the diamond's a square on point; at the bottom of the pines; spent; Putnam Valley; Golden Poverty (formerly Body of Love); stringent

www.ingramcontent.com/pod-product-compliance
Lightning Source LLC
Chambersburg PA
CBHW012101090526
44592CB00017B/2649